W. C. Morrow

1881 King of the Carnaval

W. C. Morrow

1881 King of the Carnaval

ISBN/EAN: 9783337866082

Printed in Europe, USA, Canada, Australia, Japan

Cover: Foto ©ninafisch / pixelio.de

More available books at **www.hansebooks.com**

THE KING OF THE CARNIVAL.

I.—THE QUEEN OF THE FAIRIES.

In the year 1859 there lived in the richest and proudest aristocratic settlement of the lower Mississippi Valley two young men about twenty-five years of age, named respectively Henry Le Baron and Ambrose Hunter. They were unmarried, and belonged to two of the most powerful families in the South. In truth, apart from the fact that they were men of strict honor, careful education, and unflinching bravery, their names alone would have sufficed to place them in that high position in society to which their merits entitled them; for the names Hunter and Le Baron belonged only to persons of the highest caste.

Though possessing widely differing characteristics and temperaments, they had an unusually strong attachment for each other;

and this fact had been known through all the years during which they had grown up together, studied together, and traveled together. The pleasures of one were not complete if not shared by the other. Hunter was the handsomer, and brighter, and more attractive; but Le Baron was the stronger friend, because he had the greater heart. Hunter was a conversationalist and wit; and Le Baron a thinker and philosopher.

This placid sea of friendship was, in the year above mentioned, suddenly disturbed by a pretty woman, who plunged heedlessly therein; and what at first appeared a ripple on the surface eventually became a storm, and all the dark terrors of the deep snapped their chains and hurried to the fray.

Louise came like a gleam of bright May sunshine into the quiet settlement. Innocent, rich, beautiful; overrunning with life and pathetic tenderness of heart; a born coquette; a rogue with men's happiness; she soon found at her feet the two finest young men in the country—Hunter and Le Baron. It was thought that Hunter was the more susceptible of the two; but calm men have none the less quick and open hearts, and Le Baron's love burst upon his self-consciousness at once, and came to be a part of his deep, silent nature. Yet he believed—and with good cause — that the sterner stuff of which he was made awed the little beauty, who found a boon companion in Hunter.

Under other circumstances, Le Baron would not have been the man to yield one jot or tittle to another man in a fair contest for a woman's hand; but Hunter was his friend, and he would have cut off his right hand for Hunter's sake. Indeed, that Louise preferred Hunter did not even grieve him; for, with his old-time philosophy, he reflected that Hunter's happiness was sacred, and he would not disturb it; and that there were other good and beautiful women in the world. But how was it with Hunter? Ah, different! The more impetuous and passionate, the less could he brook a hindrance or a cross. He, too, was generous, but not self-sacrificing. He could have stormed a prison and rescued

his friend at the sacrifice of his life; but he could not have gone to the dungeon in his stead. And so Hunter madly loved Louise, and never asked himself: "Does Le Baron love her?"

Let it be said of these two young men that neither was jealous of the other. Why should they be? Le Baron crushed out this feeling in his own heart, as he would stamp out any other that dishonored him; while Hunter, knowing his friend's honor, had no uneasiness of treachery. It was even with pride that he saw Le Baron's admiration of Louise, for he reflected that Le Baron was a man of infallible taste. And it may be here remarked, that Le Baron, being the deeper and sterner of the two men, and having more forethought, keener observation, and calmer judgment, exercised a strong influence over Hunter. The latter appreciated this fact; but so great was his attachment to Le Baron, that he never experienced jealousy or disquietude on that account. Even Louise, a light-hearted butterfly of to-day, saw the difference between the two men, and feared the one while she liked the other.

Louise had never seen a glimpse of Le Baron's heart. With her he was always the same calm, thoughtful, impenetrable man; and to her credit it shall be recorded, that she smothered that instinct belonging peculiarly to frivolous women, which directs them to conquer the most surly lion in the shape of a man. It is matter of daily wonder to me that the grandest hearts are so often flung away upon coquettes, while the patient, noble, self-denying women are thrust to the wall. But it shall also be said—and this time not so much to her credit—that she feared to trifle with the impetuous, unruly Hunter.

While it is commonly admitted that the weakest women rule the strongest men, I believe there never lived a greater error in fact; for when such a case is pointed out to me, I will say the man has a large heart, but a weak nature; and that the woman is a virago disguised as Folly: or, if this be not the case, I will show that the man, though using, seemingly, a long and loose halter about the woman's neck, has it securely tied, for all that; and sometimes makes it choke when she stretches it very far.

And thus the days went by; and the only ripple on the sea was a weight that hung upon Le Baron's heart. It changed him surely, but almost imperceptibly. It made the unattainable treasure more precious, and the hopelessness more painful. What if it gnawed at his vitals—could he help it? Was he blamable for feeling that Hunter's happiness jarred upon him? Could he be censured for caring less for his friend's society? There is a limit to all human endurance; but sometimes that limit is reached only at death. And thus the days went by; and thus the ripple extended from center to circumference, while submarine caverns slowly yielded up their hidden monsters, which marshaled secretly and in lower darkness.

The two friends became gradually estranged. Le Baron manfully struggled against it; but when Hunter would chide him he could not resist the temptation to plead unusual press of study. Then he would take Hunter's hand, and assure him that they were as good friends as ever; and Hunter would leave him with a light heart—all unsuspecting—to see Louise.

The world soon said that Hunter and Louise would marry. Le Baron had schooled himself to contemplate that possibility face to face; to realize it beforehand; to seek consolation in his philosophy and his friend's happiness. But not once did he mention the subject to Hunter.

"Hal," said Hunter, one day, as he was dining with Le Baron, "have you heard this rumor about Louise and me?"

"I paid no attention to it, Ambrose."

"Ah, you are as cold-blooded as ever! The handsomest woman in the land could not tempt you away from your philosophy."

"And Louise is that fairest one, Ambrose."

"To me she is, Hal."

"And *for* you, surely?"

"Ha, ha! I hope so. But do you know that she is the veriest little witch of a coquette?—the Queen of the Fairies? You see I have to talk to you voluntarily, for you never ask me for confidences."

"I really wish you happiness, Ambrose."

"Hal, if I didn't believe that I have all her affection, I would be intensely jealous of you."

"And why, Ambrose?"

"Because she talks of you constantly, and deplores what she says is your evident dislike of her; and says that such great, strong lions as you never seem to have wit enough to know that they can command any woman like a slave, and crush her like a lily—"

"Ambrose," exclaimed Le Baron, holding up his hand, "that is enough!"

"—that any woman prefers a man who will be her master, to one who will be her companion. And do you know, Hal, that I think one reason why the little beauty loves me is because she fears me!"

"Doubtless, Ambrose."

"You will be at the ball to-night, I suppose, Hal?"

"Yes; I think so."

And they parted. Then Le Baron got up and stretched himself, like a tired mastiff. Then he went to a mirror and surveyed himself calmly. An indefinable feeling had taken possession of him, and it tugged at his heart unmercifully. He could not understand it, and hence could not face it. It was the mouth of a cave—an illimitable darkness—that yawned at his feet. Like a brave man, and a strong, and a good, he sought to banish it. He was startled to find an unnatural color in his cheeks. His hands were cold, and his heart beat fast. It was the agony of a strong, stern man. He tried to read, and failed; and then he reflected that the last knotty point he had discovered in international law was wearying, and his mind could not grasp it. In fact, he had studied hard all day. Consequently, all that he needed was rest.

II.—THE MONSTERS OF THE DEEP.

The ball was a brilliant affair. The two friends were there, and Louise. She greeted Le Baron warmly, and chided him for his recent neglect of her; but his manner was more constrained than ever; and she ran away from him. He chatted with some ladies, lounged in the cloak-room, smoked on the veranda, and strolled alone through the grounds. After Louise deserted him, he had not glanced once in her direction; and she felt (watching him constantly) that she was not, and never would be, the subject of a single thought of his. But what a grand thing it would be to conquer such a proud, stern heart!—and what a treasure that heart must be!

Suddenly, while walking in the grounds, he was startled by a soft rustling; and before he could turn, a bare, round, dimpled arm was thrust through his.

"Ah, I've caught you moping!" laughed gay Louise.

Perhaps for the first time in his life Le Baron was seriously embarrassed.

"You see," she ran on, not giving him time to speak, "Ambrose is dancing and flirting with that doll-face blonde (*I* don't think she's so very pretty); and then, it is so terribly warm in there; and so I ran out just to find you; just to find you—think of that! And I knew you didn't want me about you—you are so cross with me, and never have a kind word for me, and —"

And here she actually choked with a sob!

"Louise!"

"Oh, you don't deny it, and you can't! And so I made up my mind to do the meanest and wickedest thing in my power, and that is to tease you, and make you hate me still more."

"Louise! I—"

"Now don't say a word. Don't perjure yourself. Gracious! I am freezing! Will you *never* go and get me a wrap! and will you *ever* ask me to have an ice? Don't you see I'm nearly dead?"

"Pardon me, Louise; come."

Shaking out her skirts, she took his arm, and they repaired to the refreshment-room, she talking all the while as if her very life depended on it; and, upon my honor, I believe it did. When they had reached the door she suddenly drew back, and said:

"Look at my face."

"Well, it is very pretty."

"Nonsense! I mean, do I look as if I had been crying?"

"Somewhat," he replied, so indifferently that it cut her to the heart; and her eyes filled afresh. Seeing it, he stooped, and said softly:

"Ambrose should not treat you so ill."

Ambrose, indeed!

They sat down to the dainties; and so volubly did she chat, while she avoided his look, that he wondered if she had a heart; and thought how easy it would be for a good man to wreck his life on a rock hidden beneath such a hope. But ah! she was very, very pretty, and very weak! You should have a strong, tender hand to guide you, little Queen; for your subjects, the fairies, are merely for the sunshine. Beware, my true and tried friend, Le Baron! for the strength of a human heart is its greatest weakness—and so, beware!

They strolled again into the grounds, and he drew her into a summer-house, dimly lighted with Chinese lanterns in the foliage. They stood, and she chatted on and on, and never once looked into his face; and her womanly tenderness and delicacy wrought upon him strangely, while the aroma from a flower she wore crept into his brain. Ah, the world has no idea how many marriages come from a judicious use of flowers and perfumery!

Presently he took her dainty hand in his, and caressed it tenderly, while she chatted incessantly; while she told him in many words that men are *so* stupid; while she insisted that a man ought to treat a woman kindly, even if she *were* inferior to him, and even if he *did* despise her; while she argued that because a woman is weak, and didn't have any sense, she nevertheless had a great deal of heart—oh, yes! in fact she did; while she said that some women—and it was quite natural with a great many—could hide their true feelings from *any* man they admired, and sometimes flirted with other men through sheer perverseness, and that men are *so* stupid that they *never* see anything, and don't know any more about a woman than the man in the moon; while she talked on and on, and went, with her whole kingdom of fairies, straight into his heart, and established her empire there, driving the Friend away; until he clasped her in his arms, and kissed her passionately, while she clung to him.

"I have always loved you, Louise!"

They were startled by a hoarse, harsh, grating voice:

"You are a traitor, Le Baron!"

Pale, haggard, his eyes starting from their sockets, his hands clenched, trembling in every joint, Ambrose Hunter stood in the door, and hurled that insult at Le Baron.

Louise shrunk back. The fairies, which, until then, had been flitting about, hurried away in dire consternation, deserting their Queen; and in their stead came the monsters of the deep; for the storm was loud, and shipwreck inevitable.

Le Baron turned deathly pale. Indeed, he felt himself a traitor. Hunter glared at Louise, who shrunk away from him, and cowered speechless on a seat.

"Henry Le Baron, what have you to say? I denounce you as a villain and a traitor!"

Le Baron mutely pointed to Louise, but Hunter gave no heed. His words were loud and angry. His condition was the insanity of rage—blasted hope—treachery—humiliation. His tones attracted some strollers, who gathered about with frightened faces. He turned to these; and in a haughty, imperious manner, said:

"Mark you! that man, who said he was my friend, is a villain!—mark it well."

He was nervously unbuttoning his right glove, and slipping it from his hand.

"Mark it well, I tell you!—he is a villain of the lowest kind!"

He had removed the glove. Quick as a panther, and in the desperation of uncontrollable rage, he sprang at Le Baron, and dealt him a stinging blow with the open hand upon his face.

The blow descended upon Le Baron like a thunderbolt. His face mantled, and then changed to the hue of death. Still he did not move. His chest heaved, but that was

all. Hunter glared at him with the fury of a mad beast. Taking the glove from a table on which he had thrown it, he hurled it full in Le Baron's face. It struck and fell to the ground.

"I call upon you, men and women," continued Hunter, "to mark the insult for which nothing but death can atone. See how the craven traitor trembles! What! will he add the infamy of cowardice to the infamy of treachery? Will he not accept the glove?"

Le Baron's eyes had from the first been riveted on Hunter's scornful face. He was very pale. Slowly and deliberately and without a word, he picked up the glove, carefully brushed a little loose dirt from it, smoothed out the wrinkles, folded it neatly, and put it into his pocket. Then it was death—nothing but death.

Hunter, seeing that the gage was taken up, scornfully turned on his heel and walked away, without even glancing at Louise, who cowered on the seat, weeping, crushed, and broken. Some persons attempted to address her and Le Baron; but he proudly waved them away, and was then left alone with the fallen Queen, whose every subject had deserted her. But little could have passed between them, for a man with a blow upon the cheek had no right to address a lady. However, it was a fact, remarked at the time as strange, that he left her an old man—aimless, hopeless, looking no one in the face, speaking to none—not a trace in his face of the joyful look of a successful suitor.

The next day Hunter, exasperated at the delay of the expected challenge, sent one himself. Le Baron quietly remarked to the messenger:

"I shall call upon your principal in half an hour."

"Then you do not accept?"

"I have nothing more to say to you, sir."

This man left. At the appointed time Le Baron was announced at Hunter's residence. Hunter, apprised of his approach, had him met at the door by the friend, who informed him that Hunter would see him under no circumstances until the final meeting.

"Bah!" exclaimed Le Baron, as he thrust the friend aside and stalked into the room.

Hunter arose, the old anger banishing from his face an unusual pallor.

"You dare, sir, to enter my house?"

"Be quiet, Hunter; I have something to say to you."

"Say nothing to me, sir! My friend is in the hall—speak to him."

"Nevertheless, I shall speak to you."

As Le Baron made this reply in a calm, sorrowful voice, he seated himself, and motioned to Hunter to do likewise; and so great was his assurance, and so evident his superior nerve and self-control, that, yielding to the old influence of his friend, Hunter dropped helplessly into his chair, still scornful and defiant.

"Hunter, you think I am a traitor—"

"*Think*, sir?"

"Be quiet, if you please."

This sudden rejoinder, accompanied by a dark and terrible look, though it did not frighten or intimidate the dauntless Hunter, made it evident that Le Baron had a powerful motive in seeking the interview—a motive that must have been of the greatest power, that so proud and fearless a man as Le Baron should thus have come to him, with the blow still burning his cheek like fire.

"You think I am a traitor," continued Le Baron, calmly. "I do not blame you. I find no fault with you for the rash and desperate step you took last night. It was natural. You thought I had deliberately planned it all. Well, you have passed an insult upon me of a nature that, under ordinary circumstances, no man having a drop of honorable blood in his veins could live under. It would be an easy matter to resent it—to fight you—to kill you, or be killed by you. Nothing is simpler. All that is required is a little brute courage, which we both, unfortunately, possess too bountifully. To do otherwise would require a more manly courage, which I believe we both possess. The case is extraordinary. It has been many months since my affection for you was as strong as it is now. I formed a preference—we will say, love—for this heartless, frivolous woman, as soon as you did, Ambrose. You see I am perfectly candid with you. I could not let one of us die without this full understanding. I conquered my love, because I saw that you loved her; and I never put forth the least effort to win her regard. When you think of it calmly, you will admit that. Last night I unconsciously yielded to the influence of her loveliness. That my regard for her should for a single moment have caused me to forget you, the friend and companion of a lifetime, Ambrose, was evidence to me, after a night of careful thought, that it is poisonous and pernicious. Ambrose, this woman is lost to you; she is also lost to me."

Hunter looked sullenly at the floor. Le Baron continued:

"If ever I loved her, I do not now. She tried her power upon me, and succeeded in degrading me and losing me my only friend. I know her now. My eyes are opened. A revulsion of feeling for her has ensued. She can never be my wife. Ambrose, shall this heartless flirt make sport of strong men, and brave men, and set them upon each other like dogs? Would it not be too great a victory for her, Ambrose? Is she worthy the sacrifice of a good man's life? And if that life is taken, who is benefited? I put it to your heart and reason calmly, Ambrose—I, who am the one bearing the stain—I, who carry the blow upon my cheek."

Such magnanimity was deeper than the farthest depths of Hunter's heart; and the appeal, though it touched him, caused even that fleeting feeling to alarm him; and he answered scornfully—doubly injured that his friend seemed greater than he:

"Are you through, sir?—and do you intend to live under the disgrace?"

"Ambrose, it is not you that speaks. Ambrose, I am your old-time friend Hal. Let us forget it all, Ambrose. Take my hand, my boy."

He had advanced to Hunter with extended hand; but the latter thrust it roughly aside, and said, harshly:

"As a winner of the prize, you can well afford to proffer your friendship, and make a fool and a laughing-stock of me. You would not shock your lady-love with a hole in your breast. I scorn your friendship, as I despise the puritanical hypocrisy of your face and words."

Le Baron was stunned with grief.

"Then it is all over between us," he said.

"There is but one thing necessary."

"The duel?"

"Yes."

"I shall not fight you."

"What!" exclaimed Hunter, springing to his feet in astonishment. "Are you indeed a coward?"

Le Baron made no reply.

"I shall publish you as a coward," said Hunter.

"Very good."

"And you will not resent it?"

"No."

"Ah!" exclaimed Hunter, "I understand you now! Your Louise—your loving Louise—has made you promise not to fight, and hence you degraded yourself by coming to me to-day! I dare you to deny it, sir!"

Le Baron made no reply, but started, crushed and sorrowful, toward the door.

"That confirms my suspicions. You are a poltroon as well as a knave. You give up your manhood for a woman's embrace. Well, other men have done it. Very well, sir; let the proud name of Le Baron be forever disgraced by the cowardice of a Le Baron. There is the door, sir."

Without another word Le Baron left, an old, broken man. On the same day Hunter placarded him as a coward and traitor, warning all honest men and good women against him. That night Le Baron disappeared. Hunter remained at home, a moody, silent man, seeing no one. After two weeks the news reached him that Louise had died of brain-fever and a broken heart; and then he left home; soon afterward he went to the war, in which he remained to the close, winning the stars of a Brigadier-General for valor on the field; and then, without returning home, he went to Europe, and was not heard of again.

III.—THE KING AND THE KNIGHT.

Ten years had passed since the scene in the summer-house transpired, and the morning of Mardi Gras dawned in Mobile. Felix, King of the Carnival, had long ago issued his imperial decree calling upon his faithful subjects throughout his glorious kingdom to assemble in the City of the Gulf, the Mother of Mystics, on this, the Day of Joy, there to hold high carnival to please his Most Gracious Majesty. And right loyally had they obeyed, for the quaint old city was crowded with visitors. As early as ten o'clock in the forenoon, masquers appeared upon the streets in all manner of gay costumes. It had been announced by imperial proclamation that his Majesty, the good King Felix, with the members of his royal household, would enter the city by the Eastern Gate, where he would be met by his faithful servant, his Honor, the Mayor, accompanied by the City Fathers in regalia of state, and a battalion of mounted police, and the several military companies, and other subjects of low and high degree.

The royal cavalcade, as it approached the Eastern Gate, was an imposing spectacle. All were in gorgeous costumes. First came the King's Herald, and then the buglers; next, the Royal Lancers, magnificently mounted; next, the Royal Guard, also mounted, and with drawn swords; next, the good King himself, drawn in a golden chariot by twelve proud black horses in gilt harness; next, the members of the King's household, outriders, pages, guards, and other subjects.

The two cavalcades approached each other. The Mayor and City Fathers advanced on foot. The venerable King left his chariot, and ascended a throne erected on a miniature Field of the Cloth of Gold. The Mayor knelt at the throne, and delivered into the hands of his Imperial Majesty an impossible gilt key three feet long, which betokened the surrender of the city by right to the imaginary Eastern Gate. His Honor, accompanying the presentation with an address of welcome, formally turned over to his Aristocratic Majesty the city of his Majesty's choice, with the subjects therein, and the military and police, with full power over persons and property. The King replied. Cannon were fired, and all the bells pealed gladly; and it was known far and wide that Felix, King of the Carnival, had assumed possession of the city.

Who was this mock king for a day—this haughty, stern, imperial Felix. There were few who knew. It is always kept a secret from the common people. He is chosen for a day. Mysticism and mummery are indispensable. On this occasion the King was, as is usual, a venerable man, whose white beard extended below his waist; and with shaggy grey eyebrows, and long white hair. Yet beneath this trickery of false hair was a pair of vigorous, massive shoulders, and a stature tall, strong, and erect—a typical king.

The knowing ones said he was none other than the great lawyer, Gaston—a poor man who had fought as a common soldier in the war; a strange, reticent, shrinking man, yet one whose cool daring had suppressed the riots; a man who avoided society, and who was never known to speak to a lady; a man whose great talents and profound learning, together with his uniform gentleness, modesty, and honesty, had, in spite of him, made him honored and sought for; a man who had firmly put aside all opportunities for winning easy renown as a statesman, but who pursued his own quiet way, making friends unconsciously, and almost unwillingly. And against his protest he had been chosen King of the Carnival.

The King and his train moved upon the heart of the city to head the grand parade that would there be formed. The streets were now packed with merry masquers. All restraints of deportment and caste were thrown aside, and the devil hobnobbed with the angels. Perhaps one or two tragedies had been enacted, when a masquer slipped a knife between an enemy's ribs, and then disappeared in the crowd. All had yielded to the mad intoxication of the hour.

Among the gay knights who, walking or mounted, passed hither and thither, was a handsome stranger-knight, finely mounted. He wore no masque. He had iron-grey hair, piercing black eyes, and a black mustache and imperial, both prematurely tinged with grey. He attracted marked attention for his handsome face, graceful carriage, and costly equipage.

This stranger-knight, seeing that the King had come, put spurs to his horse, dashed through the cordon of guards and outriders that surrounded the King's chariot, drew his sword, and cried in a loud, insulting voice, that thrilled every breast:

"Ho! you false, dishonored King! Ho! all you people!—your King bears a blow upon his cheek, and a stain upon his name! He dishonored his manhood and his family! He makes fools of you all, and insults you with his presence! *That* for your coward King!" and with that he struck King Felix on the breast with the flat of his sword.

Wild consternation ensued. The King seemed stunned, and sat motionless and silent.

"Ho, ho!" cried the knight; "your King trembles before a man whom he wronged. Your false King is a coward!"

The King recovered himself with a mighty effort. A crowd rushed forward to eject the intruder, but the King sternly commanded them to stand back. He stood erect in his chariot, laid aside his scepter, threw off his gorgeous robe of purple and gold; and, except as to his crown, which he retained, appeared in the elegant dress of a courtier, with his sword at his side. Then he addressed the crowd in a firm, loud voice as follows:

"Ten years ago I lived in Louisiana. My name then was Le Baron. This man was my friend and neighbor. A quarrel grew up between us. He slapped my face, and because I did not fight him he branded me as a coward. I fled the country and changed my name. The obligation that then restrained me from vindicating my honor has since been absolved by death. And now I will fight this boasting knight; and, under the duel name of King Felix and Henry Le Baron, I will remove the stain from my name."

He stepped from the chariot. The knight dismounted. There was a hush upon the crowd as of death. Interference was out of the question. The King's word was law; and the King had said he would fight.

"Do we fight with swords, Sir Knight?" he asked.

"As you please," haughtily replied the other.

The King's eyes were bright, and the old look of weariness and sadness gave place to one of joy. They approached each other with drawn swords.

"Guard carefully, false King," said the knight, tauntingly. "I warn you that you must guard well; for in Paris I have handled the sword since you and I studied with the foils there fifteen years ago."

The King guarded, and the swords were crossed, and the click of the steel sent a chill around.

At this moment a pale, frightened woman tried to push her way through the crowd, and she begged the bystanders to stop the fight. They made way for her—she pressed forward, calling upon them in God's name to stop the fight. But her feeble voice was drowned in the hum that arose, and she fell fainting, and was borne away.

With a pass that was quick and bold, the knight displayed his superior skill by striking the crown from the King's head, causing his long white hair to stream in the wind. The King redoubled his caution, and fought on the defensive. The sword, long unused, was awkward in his hand.

"Have a care, Le Baron!" cried the impetuous Hunter. "I have killed my man with the sword. Remember that this has no button on the point."

Le Baron made no reply, but maintained a cautious guard. Hunter continued his taunts:

"Guard your head, man, or I'll lay it open!"

The King fought solely on the defensive and in this he apparently had all he could do. He saw that Hunter was playing with him, and that the knight intended to run him through when sufficient time should have

been consumed to give the affair the poor semblance of a fair duel. But his guard improved so rapidly that the furious knight saw he must make short work of it. He gave a skillful thrust, which was parried. There was heard the wiry slipping of steel upon steel, cold and smooth. The King was perfectly cool, and resigned to death; while the knight, failing again and again, became exasperated, and redoubled the fury of the assault. The King no longer gave way, but stood his ground. On the one hand the work was hot and furious; on the other, patient, careful, watchful—nay, sorrowful.

Suddenly the King reeled; the blood started from his breast. His assailant pursued the advantage, crowding him, and fighting madly. The King's false grey beard was torn away. The knight's sword, made for dueling, was long, thin, and elastic; the King's, gold-mounted and made for ornament, was white, dead, unyielding, and clumsy; but it had the advantage of greater weight. The King became deathly white. Not a single cut or thrust had he attempted. The knight, to test him, opened a way to his breast; but the King pretended not to see it. Did the knight understand this greatness of heart? No; it maddened him! The King's knees trembled. His blood streamed upon the ground from many wounds. And still he parleyed with death, hoping Hunter's heart would melt.

The King staggered, and dropped, exhausted, to his knees.

"You court death, do you?" cried the knight, as he rushed blindly upon the wounded King. "Then you shall have it!" But his haste and madness were too great. His foot slipped in the blood, and he fell upon the extended sword of the King, which ran him through the heart.

A pale woman in black—the same who had sought to prevent the deed—placed a wreath of flowers, wet with her tears, upon the grave of Ambrose Hunter, and prayed there alone: and it was she who was the most faithful among the constant watchers at Le Baron's bedside during the long days of fever and delirium that followed the duel. But though women whispered among themselves mysteriously, she was at the bedside every day; and the men there did not molest her, nor seek to pry into the reason. When no one else was near she would cover the hand of the unconscious man with kisses, and on her knees pray at his bedside for his recovery. But when at last Le Baron regained consciousness, she disappeared without his having seen her, and never came back again. They told him of her; and, greatly wondering and deeply touched, he did, when he was well and strong again, have her sought and found. And then he went to her—for now he could look a good woman in the face—and she stood before him humbly, in the pale beauty and loveliness that years and sorrow had tempered and refined—the Queen of the Fairies of old.

"Louise!" he exclaimed.

She fell at his feet, and groveled there, weeping with joy. He raised her in his strong arms, and kissed her; and neither could speak for some time. Then there was an explanation—she had sent out the rumor of her death after a dangerous illness, that it might soften Hunter toward his friend; she had sought Le Baron far and wide, and had found him a year ago, and had silently watched over him ever since.

"And though I was bitter against you, at first, Louise," he said, "your sweet face haunted me through all the dreary years; and long ago I ceased to think of you as a coquette; but I revered your sweet memory, and it made me a better man."

All the fairies came trooping in—fleeing, flitting fairies!—and held high carnival; and surely in their mad frolic they must have bewitched the wedding-bells, which afterward rang so joyously!　　W. C. MORROW.

www.ingramcontent.com/pod-product-compliance
Lightning Source LLC
Chambersburg PA
CBHW031158090426
42738CB00008B/1389